Pocahontas and the settlers of Jamestown

Written by
Chris Beech

Designed by
Lucy Thuo

Illustrations by
Olexandra Sirko
and
Yaroslava Bykova

Written by Chris Beech
Book design by Lucy Thuo
Cover and character illustrations by Olexandra Sirko
Maps and Yeoman's Cottage illustrated by Yaroslava Bykova
All other illustrations thanks to Canva Pro

Copyright © Thuo Books, 2025
Text Copyright © Chris Beech, 2025
Original Artwork Copyright
© Olexandra Sirko, 2025 & © Yaroslava Bykova, 2025

All rights reserved.
No part of this book can be reproduced in any form or by written, electronic or mechanical, including photocopying, recording, or by any information retrieval system without written permission in writing by the copyright owners.

Published by Thuo Books
printed by Ingram Spark

Although every precaution has been taken in the preparation of this book, the publisher and author assume no responsibility for errors or omissions. Neither is any liability assumed for damages resulting from the use of information contained herein.

ISBN 978-1-7392917-9-2

Contents page

Longing to leave	7
Venturing out	8
To the New World	9
Before the settlers	10
Playful one	11
The Fort at Jamestown	12
Settling in	13
Meeting Powhatan	14
Sharing supplies	15
Mapping the Chesapeake Bay	16
John Smith's rude response	17
Bermuda	18
John Smith's incident	19
Kocoum and Pocahontas	20
Pocahontas is kidnapped	21
Pocahontas is baptised	22
John Rolfe and Pocahontas	23
Pocahontas travels to England	24
Pocahontas gets a royal welcome	25
Pocahontas meets John Smith again	26
Pocahontas's last journey	27

Longing to leave

By the time John Smith was thirteen, he longed to be an explorer like his hero Sir Francis Drake, who had sailed around the world. John's father was prospering as a yeoman farmer in Lincolnshire and expected his son to forget such ideas and settle down to a life like his. As John could not convince his father to let him follow his dream, he tried to run away from home several times but he was always brought back. His father eventually apprenticed him to a merchant to keep him busily employed and out of mischief. However, in 1596 (when John was 16) his father died and he left his apprenticeship and set off on his adventures.

Did you know?
A yeoman was ranked lower than a gentleman but above a commoner.

Venturing out

John Smith fought in other nations' wars as a mercenary. He was shipwrecked and rescued by a pirate ship, so for a while, he joined the pirates and became wealthy. However, he left this life and went back to fighting. At one city surrounded by enemies, John fought consecutive duels with three champion fighters of the enemy, each using different weapons. Each time he was victorious and so was honoured for his bravery and skill by the Prince of Transylvania, who made him an English gentleman. He was also promoted and became Captain John Smith. Later he fought in a battle but was injured and left for dead. His enemies rescued him and sold him into slavery. One day when his master was treating him particularly cruelly, John got so fed up that he overpowered his master, took his clothes and escaped into the desert. Eventually, he made his way home after travelling across many countries.

To the New World

When John Smith reached England, he heard that the Virginia Company was planning to send colonists to the New World (the Americas). John longed to be part of this expedition and made friends with the key people who could help him to be chosen, including the explorer and privateer Bartholomew Gosnold. John set out on the *Susan Constant*, one of three ships of settlers, along with the *Godspeed* and the *Discovery*. The journey took much longer than expected: five months instead of one. When they stopped at Nevis in the West Indies, Captain Newport hastily got gallows built for John, having accused him of trying to take control during the voyage. John had spent some of the journey chained up as a prisoner. Luckily for John, when Newport wanted to kill him, Bartholomew Gosnold, captain of the *Godspeed*, and a priest came to his rescue. It must have been a shock to everyone when they finally opened their sealed orders after reaching Virginia to see that John Smith was named as one of the council members.

Before the settlers

When the settlers reached the New World, they were far from alone. Many Native American tribes inhabited it. Although each tribe had its own chief, most of the native people the settlers met were under the rule of Chief Powhatan, known as the Chief of Chiefs. Powhatan's father had previously ruled over six tribes. As chief, Powhatan extended his control to cover 30 tribes and around 10,000 square miles. When the settlers arrived, he was a tall, imposing man, approximately 60 years old. Powhatan was strict and formidable so his people were careful not to upset him, fearing his punishments.

Playful one

Although Powhatan was to be feared, his people also greatly respected him. He had many children, but his favourite daughter was the 11 year old he nicknamed Pocahontas, which can mean 'Playful one'. Even though she was the much-loved daughter of such a powerful chief, Pocahontas would still have had many chores to do as she learned the skills needed to be a grown woman. By the time she was 13, Pocahontas would have had to know how to cook, pick edible wild plants, grow and harvest their crops and deal with what the hunters caught. Pocahontas would also have to understand how to care for children, build a home, make mats, pots and clothes and cut men's hair. Despite all these tasks, Pocahontas was full of fun and mischief and she loved doing cartwheels.

The River James

The Fort at Jamestown

The settlers found the site of what would become Jamestown and decided it was ideal as a harbour for their ships and a great location to defend against colonists from other European countries. However, problems came from local tribes who attacked their settlement. In response, they built a fort with walls in a triangle around a church, storehouse and houses, with cannons facing out from the corners to protect them from attack.

Settling in

As well as being in an excellent position to defend against enemies, the site of Jamestown must have seemed like a perfect choice to the settlers as it was uninhabited. However, they soon discovered why this was the case. The ground was marshy and difficult to farm and the place was swarming with mosquitoes. Getting suitable drinking water also became a problem. The water tasted sweet in the spring, as it was added to by melted snow from the mountains. However, as the weather got hotter the saltwater moved further up the estuary, making the water at Jamestown five times too salty for humans to drink safely. The settlers relied on trading goods for food with local tribes, but they too were struggling to feed their people. Further adding to their struggle, the settlers arrived after planting season at the start of a severe seven-year drought, the worst in almost 800 years.

Meeting Powhatan

John Smith was a very practical man who realised the need to trade with the local tribes for food. He also wanted to explore the area. He led an exploration up the Chickahominy River, where Native Americans ambushed him and his men and took John to Powhatan. At first, John seemed to be an honoured guest, having been given a bowl of water to wash his hands and then a bunch of feathers to dry them. However, after sharing in a feast, there was a long discussion between Powhatan and other chiefs, after which they placed two huge stones down. John was dragged over and had his head laid on the stones, with other men threatening him with their clubs. He feared that they were about to kill him. Suddenly, Pocahontas ran forward and laid her head over his to protect him. Powhatan then became friendly again, wanting to trade with John and his people.

Sharing supplies

However, John Smith's own people were less willing to accept him on his return. One man in particular, Gabriel Archer, was convinced that John was responsible for the loss of his companions and demanded his life as payment. John was about to be hanged when Pocahontas arrived with food and provisions from John's new friend Powhatan, which not only rescued John from being hanged but also saved many settlers from starvation. Another lifeline came in the form of the first supply ships led by Captain Newport and Captain Francis Nelson. They brought ample supplies and a hundred new men, which greatly propped up the depleted colony. They also took some of John's greatest enemies, including Gabriel Archer, back to England. However, the new colonists were inexperienced. One accidentally set fire to Jamestown, destroying all the homes, meaning the colonists had to work hard to rebuild what they had lost in the freezing January frost. Powhatan sent Pocahontas with supplies of food and clothes to help them at this difficult time.

Mapping the Chesapeake Bay

On 2nd June 1608, John Smith started one of his explorations of the Chesapeake Bay. On this trip, he noticed some fish in shallow waters and set about spearing them with the tip of his sword. He was very successful until one such fish turned out to be a stingray that stung him on his wrist, leaving him in so much pain that he got his men to dig him a grave. However, Dr Russell, who had been accompanying him on the trip, managed to revive John so much that he felt well enough to enjoy eating the stingray for dinner. The location has since been known as Stingray Point.

Did you Know?

During these explorations of Virginia and later ones of New England, John created highly accurate maps, which were actively used for seven decades and were a great help to explorers.

John Smith's rude response

In September 1608, John Smith became President of Jamestown. He took a firm, practical approach to organising the colony, insisting that everyone had to work to be fed unless they were sick or disabled. Previously, everyone could have food from a common storehouse. He organised military training and ensured the settlers dug a well, planted crops and fished for food. Whereas many settlers starved before and after his time as president, no one died of starvation during his presidency. However, the Virginia Company in London was funding these expeditions to the New World and expected riches in return. When they asked for £2,000 in gold in return for the second of the supply ships, John replied bluntly, unlike previous reports, which had given a falsely optimistic view of how things were going. He described in detail how wretched their condition was and how there was no prospect of gold. He requested more food supplies and settlers with the practical skills needed to help the colony to flourish.

Bermuda

Whatever the Virginia Company may have thought about the bluntness of John Smith's response, they took notice of his words. A third supply mission was sent, consisting of nine well-equipped ships, including a newly-built flagship, the *Sea Venture*. All went well until a few days away from Jamestown, when a severe storm hit the fleet. One ship sank. The *Sea Venture* struggled hard against the storm but it started taking on water as it was so new that its timbers had not yet set correctly. Everyone tried bailing out the water but too much was coming in. Sir George Somers was at the ship's helm and took it onto a reef rather than letting it sink in the pounding waves. Everyone (around 150 people and one dog) was saved and landed on the then-uninhabited island of Bermuda. For the next nine months, they worked hard building ships to take them on the remainder of their journey. During this time, one of the settler families, the Rolfes, gave birth to a baby girl, who they named Bermuda. Sadly, the baby did not survive and her mother died soon after. The widower, tobacco farmer John Rolfe, survived.

John Smith's incident

Even though the Virginia Company took notice of John Smith's blunt letter, they decided to replace him as president with a governor sent from England. The settlement had flourished under Smith's strict rules, but he had also made some powerful enemies. Three of these (Archer, Radcliffe and Martin) had been leading citizens in Jamestown but had returned to England after disputes with John. All three had now returned in the third supply mission, insisting that John give up his position as president, even though the newly-appointed governor Sir Thomas Gates was one of those shipwrecked on Bermuda. John refused to do this. However, one evening when he was alone on a boat, a mysterious spark set off the gunpowder stored near him. He was terribly injured and leapt into the water to ease the burning pain. He almost drowned but was rescued. When he returned to Jamestown, he was in excruciating pain and desperately needed medical attention. However, rather than sending him back to England swiftly, his enemies wanted to collect evidence and try him for all their grievances against him before they would let him go, as they knew that what happened in Virginia could not be taken to court in England. They eventually allowed him to return to England, but they would have expected him to die on the way home. Powhatan was told that he had died in the explosion. However, John survived the voyage home.

Kocoum and Pocahontas

With John Smith gone and the relationship between Powhatan and the settlers turning hostile, Pocahontas stopped visiting Jamestown for around four years. During this time, Pocahontas came to be viewed as a woman as she was 14 years old. In 1610, Pocahontas married Kocoum, who was described by one of the settlers as a private captain. He was the younger brother of Japazeus, one of the chiefs of the Patawomeck tribe, and known to be a good warrior. There had been rumours that the English wanted to capture Pocahontas. Powhatan would have thought that Kocoum's Patawomeck village, far from where the English usually ventured, would be the ideal place to hide his precious daughter.

Pocahontas is kidnapped

By this time, relations between the settlers and Powhatan had worsened and war broke out. Due to the war, Jamestown soon ran out of food and many people starved. A ship's captain, Samuel Argyll, went further afield to find a tribe friendly enough to trade. While visiting the Patawomeck tribe, he learned that Pocahontas was also there. Knowing that she was the beloved daughter of Powhatan, he decided to have her kidnapped to use as a bargaining chip to get back some of their men, weapons and tools. With a mixture of threats and promises, Argyll persuaded Japazeus to help him. Japazeus and his wife lured Pocahontas onto an English ship, pretending that his wife wanted to take a tour of it, but that he refused unless Pocahontas accompanied them. She resisted until the wife started crying. They were treated well and spent the night, but Captain Argyll's men detained Pocahontas when they tried to leave the next day. Japazeus and his wife left with the prize of a copper kettle and other trinkets in return for helping to capture her. Copper, especially if moulded, was highly prized by the Native Americans. Kocoum may have already died by this stage. If not, he would have been allowed to divorce Pocahontas after Argyll had captured her.

Pocahontas is baptised

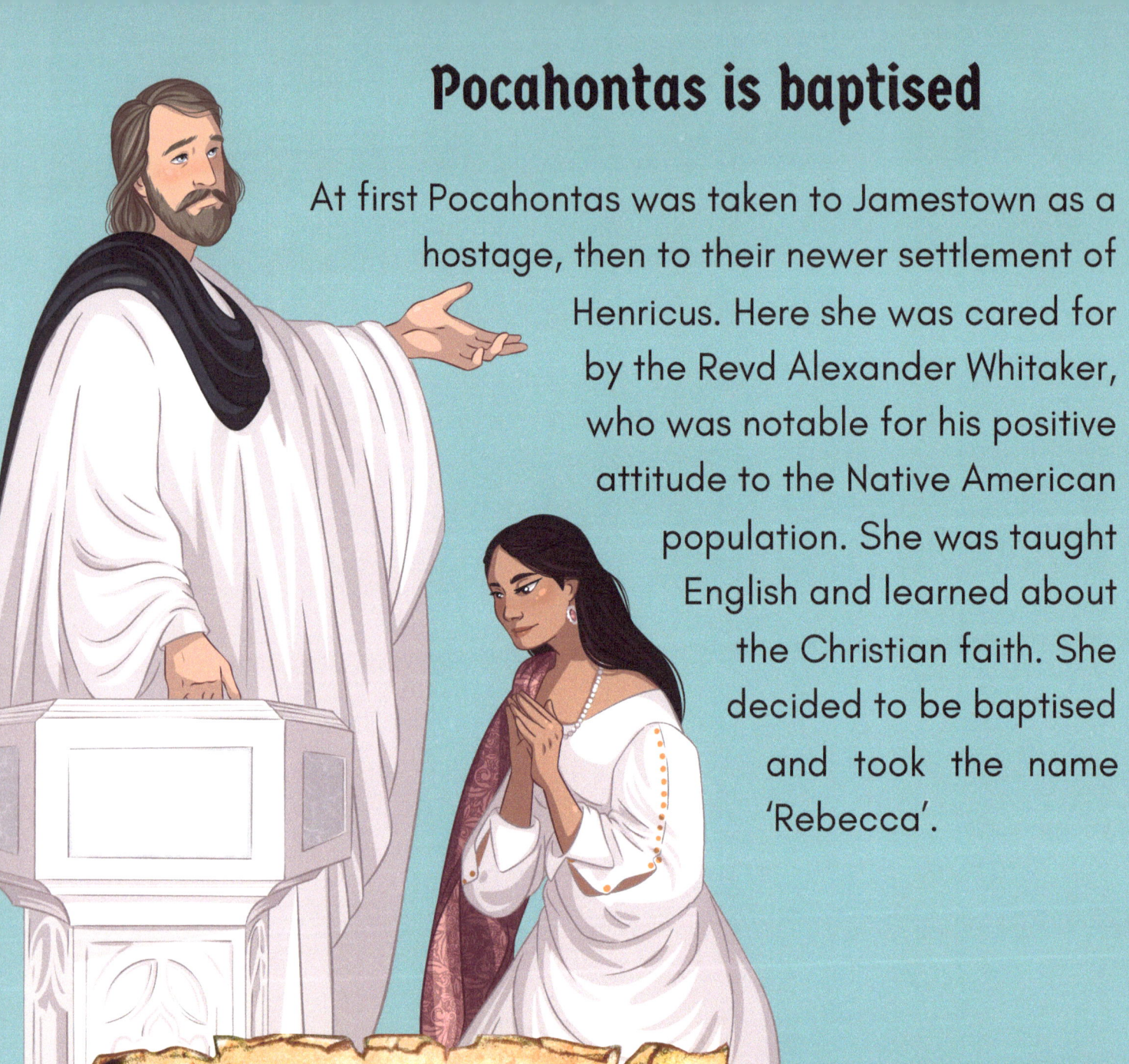

At first Pocahontas was taken to Jamestown as a hostage, then to their newer settlement of Henricus. Here she was cared for by the Revd Alexander Whitaker, who was notable for his positive attitude to the Native American population. She was taught English and learned about the Christian faith. She decided to be baptised and took the name 'Rebecca'.

Did you Know?

Sir Thomas Dale founded Henricus in 1611. It was named after the King's eldest son Henry, Prince of Wales, just as Jamestown was named after King James I. It was about 12 miles southeast of modern-day Richmond.

John Rolfe and Pocahontas

When John Rolfe arrived in Virginia from Bermuda, he brought tobacco seeds of a finer variety than that already planted by the settlers. This new type of tobacco became a very successful cash crop, which saved the settlement from financial ruin. Meeting Pocahontas, John Rolfe wanted to marry her, but he was troubled by their differences. He overcame these doubts, encouraged by her choosing to become a Christian. After getting permission to wed from Powhatan and Sir Thomas Dale, the Deputy Governor of Jamestown, Pocahontas and John Rolfe married in 1614. In 1615 she gave birth to a son, who they named Thomas. The family lived on John Rolfe's tobacco plantation at Varina Farms. Their marriage stopped the fighting between the settlers and the Native Americans and this time became known as the 'Peace of Pocahontas'.

Pocahontas travels to England

The financial success of tobacco was proving to be a turning point in the colony's success, helping to achieve the goal of making the settlement profitable. However, this raised a huge issue for the Virginia Company, since they also needed King James I's approval to continue their work. King James despised tobacco so much that he had written a book, *A Counteblaste to Tobacco*, in 1604. In this he strongly made the case that it was both harmful to health and detestable to look at and smell. The Virginia Company realised that they could gain some favour by focusing on the third point set out in the royal charter given to them by King James, suggesting that the settlers could use the trip to convert the native people of Virginia to Christianity. They had managed to accomplish this very successfully in the case of Pocahontas. Therefore, it was decided that, in the spring of 1616, Pocahontas would set sail to London with her husband, son, Sir Thomas Dale and a group of Native Americans to help generate funds for the Virginia Company and raise its profile.

Pocahontas gets a royal welcome

As the wife of a farmer, especially a tobacco farmer, Pocahontas would not have been welcome in the royal court. Indeed, John Rolfe was not invited. However, John Smith wrote a beautiful letter to Queen Anne commending Pocahontas to her as a 'Lady' and Powhatan's 'Most dear and well-beloved daughter'. He described all the times that Pocahontas's bravery and kindness in helping the English settlers had saved the colony from disaster. King James and Queen Anne took notice and Pocahontas was treated with much honour, meeting both of them during her stay. She was a special guest at a performance of Ben Jonson's  *The Vision of Delight* hosted by King James.

Pocahontas meets John Smith again

Although Pocahontas was treated well in London, she, her baby Thomas and some of her accompanying Native Americans were becoming ill. John Rolfe was worried that the air quality in London could be to blame, so they moved to Brentwood. According to local history, they also visited the Rolfe family home at Heacham. While Pocahontas was in Brentford, John Smith, at last, came to visit her. Pocahontas became overcome with emotions when she saw that John Smith was still alive; she had to go away for several hours to recover. When she returned, she told him off for not letting her know he had survived. John Smith had tried hard to return to Jamestown, but the Virginia Company had refused to allow him to go. She insisted on calling him 'Father' as Powhatan had encouraged John Smith to call him this, as a welcomed stranger in a foreign land. Although John Smith was reluctant to do so, she also asked him to call her 'Child', saying that in this way they would forever be family.

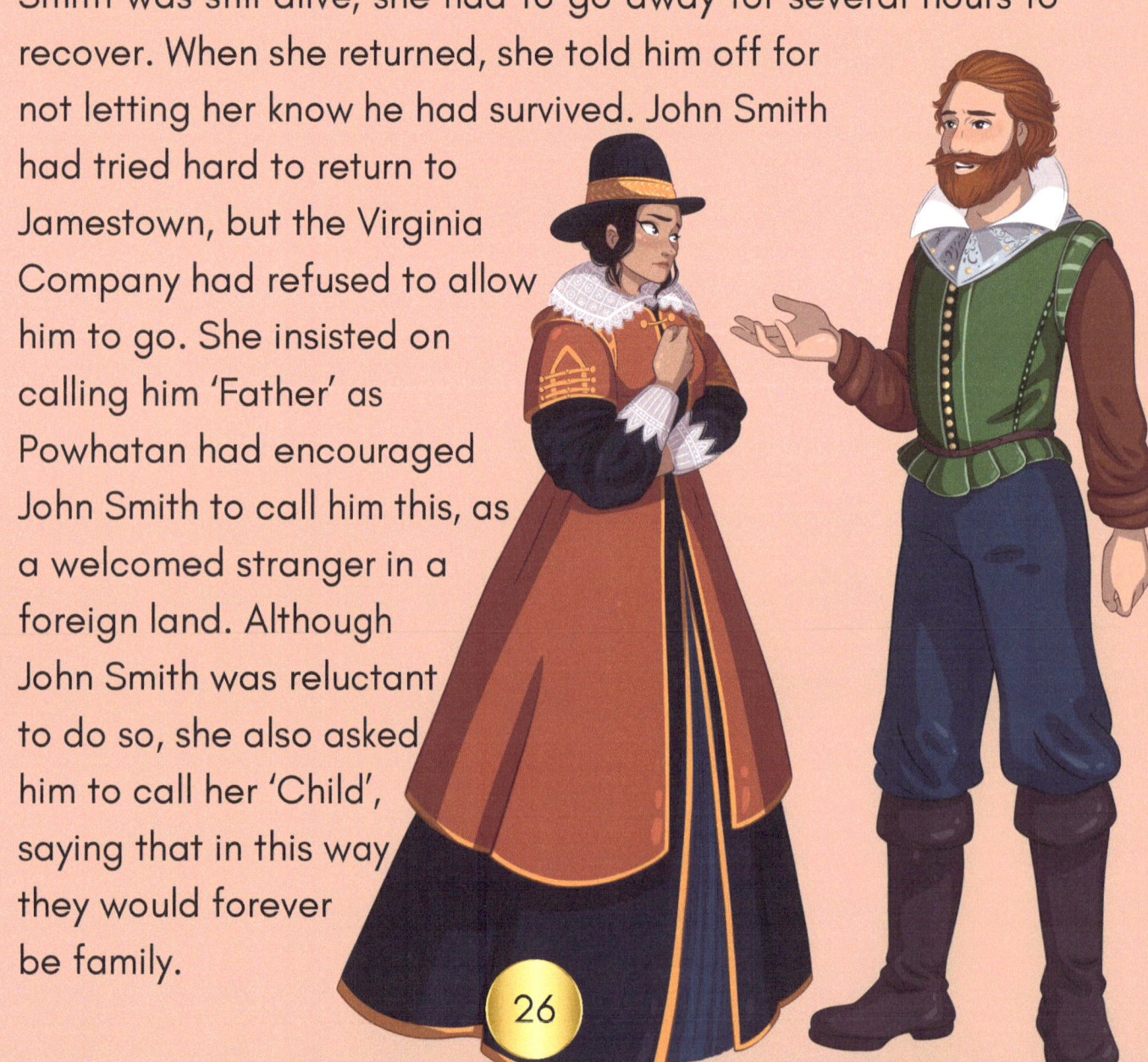

Pocahontas's last journey

John Rolfe was keen to return to his tobacco farm back in Jamestown. However, Pocahontas seemed more reluctant to leave. By the time that they set sail in March 1617, Pocahontas and baby Thomas were ill, possibly with tuberculosis or pneumonia. When they reached Gravesend, Pocahontas was dying. She was only 21 years old. Brave to the last, she comforted her husband with the words, 'All must die. It is enough that the boy liveth'. Pocahontas died and was buried at St. George's Church, which is near the River Thames in Gravesend. Her son Thomas was probably seen as too poorly to make the long voyage back to Jamestown and so was left in the care of John Rolfe's brother, to be brought up in England.

Did you Know?

Thomas survived and it is estimated that Pocahontas has tens of thousands of descendants.